MAGNIFICENT HORSES OF THE WORLD

# ANDALUSIAN HORSES

For a free color catalog describing Gareth Stevens' list of high-quality books, call 1-800-542-2595 (USA) or
1-800-461-9120 (Canada).  Gareth Stevens' Fax: (414) 225-0377.

Library of Congress Cataloging-in-Publication Data available upon request from publisher.
Fax: (414) 225-0377 for the attention of the Publishing Records Department.

ISBN 0-8368-1366-9

This edition first published in North America in 1995 by
**Gareth Stevens Publishing**
1555 North RiverCenter Drive, Suite 201
Milwaukee, Wisconsin  53212, USA

First published in Great Britain in 1994 by Sunburst Books, Deacon House, 65 Old Church Street, London, SW3 5BS.
Photographs © 1989 Franckh'sche Verlagshandlung, W. Keller & Co., Stuttgart, Germany.  Text © 1994 Sunburst Books.
Additional end matter © 1995 by Gareth Stevens, Inc.

U.S. Series Editor: Patricia Lantier-Sampon
U.S. Editor: Barbara J. Behm

Printed in China
1 2 3 4 5 6 7 8 9 9 99 98 97 96 95

MAGNIFICENT HORSES OF THE WORLD

# ANDALUSIAN HORSES

Photography by
Tomáš Míček

Text by
Dr. Hans-Jörg Schrenk

Gareth Stevens Publishing
MILWAUKEE

*Andalusian horses are at their most beautiful galloping free in the*
*meadows or along the beaches of the Atlantic coast of their*
*homelands in Spain.  Andalusians originated from*
*a historic region in southern Spain.*

An Andalusian horse is called *Caballo de Pura Raza Espanola* or "horse of pure Spanish breed." Horse lovers are enchanted by its balletic elegance, agility, high-stepping gait, and compact body. The image of fiery Andalusian stallions stepping out with decorated manes or as part of a carriage team is an unforgettable picture.

*This gray stallion sets a stark profile against the hazy rays of the setting sun.*

*A dark gray stallion lets off steam among the sand dunes of Spain's Atlantic coast.*

8

*Overleaf: A herd of Andalusian mares travels through the meadows as darkness descends. In Spain, the manes of the mares are usually clipped. Only the stallions display the full splendor of their long manes.*

In early summer, a herd of mares grazes in a meadow of grass and
herbs.  Later in the year, this land will become dry and parched
in the blazing sun.

*A stallion romances a mare.*

As long ago as 200 B.C., at the time of the Roman conquests in and around Spain, these superb horses inhabited Andalusia. They were reported to be superior to all other breeds in the Roman Empire. Later, the Moorish conquerors, who ruled Spain for about 700 years, also admired these horses. The Moors crossbred the native Spanish horses with their own Arabian and Berber breeds. After the Moors were driven from Spain in the fifteenth century, Andalusians increased in popularity. All the royal courts of Europe considered Andalusians to be the best parade horses in existence.

*This mare is keeping watch over her foal, which is just a few hours old.*

The Andalusian has had a great influence on almost all other European horse breeds. The Lipizzaner, Kladruber, Friesian, Neapolitan, and Fredericksborg breeds are directly descended from the Andalusian. Many Andalusians were taken to the Americas following numerous Spanish conquests there. Consequently, many Central, South, and North American horses can be traced back to the Andalusian breed. When it became fashionable in Spain to cross heavier, foreign horses with the Andalusians, an order of monks opposed the practice. It is thanks to these monks that the ancient, pure line of the Andalusians was preserved. All the pure Spanish Andalusians can be traced back to the horse-breeding policies of these monks. Today, purebred Andalusians are much in demand and bred throughout the world.

*This foal is of Spanish-Anglo-Arabian heritage. The crossing of Andalusians with English and Arabian thoroughbreds brings out the features of each breed that are desired in a riding horse.*

*The Andalusian has a large head; broad forehead; muscular neck; long, sloping shoulders; and low-set tail.*

Today, the main Andalusian breeding areas are in southern Spain in the region of Andalusia itself. The number of breeding areas outside Spain is also on the increase; for example, Andalusians are bred in America and Australia. In Germany, there is an association devoted to breeding Andalusians according to the aims and regulations of pure Spanish heritage.

*This Andalusian stallion senses an interesting smell. He throws his head back and flares his nostrils to detect the source.*

*One of the distinctive features of the Andalusians of pure Spanish breed is a long, silky, flowing mane.*

*A gray stallion against a foreground of golden flowers. In spring and early summer, the fields of Andalusia where the horses are raised are covered in a stunning, colorful carpet of wildflowers.*

The breeding of Andalusians is monitored by the Spanish government in Madrid. The regulations are very strict. For a foal to be awarded an official certificate, it must be presented before a government commission. When the horses are three years old, they again have to be presented before the commission. The young horses are then judged on appearance, gait, and temperament. Any horse that does not pass the examination cannot be registered or used in breeding.

*A black Andalusian stallion is an unusual sight. Gray is the most common color of the purebred Spanish horses, followed by bay.*

The breeding standards of the purebred Spanish Andalusian describe the horse as medium sized, with a straight or slightly convex profile, and a lively gait with high knee action. The head should be of medium length with well-set ears and large, expressive eyes. The neck should also be of medium length and slightly curved. Legs should be straight.

*Andalusians are about 61-63 inches (155-160 cm) tall. Their tails are low-set, and they have powerful, rounded hindquarters.*

Not only is the Andalusian enjoyed for its beauty and graceful movement, but also for its peaceful temperament. Despite the fiery impression it makes, this horse is quite docile and affectionate toward people. Andalusians are good natured and intelligent. They want to please the rider, doing whatever movement he or she asks.

*Andalusians obey the commands of their riders, but also enjoy galloping freely.*

*A play-fight between two young stallions.*

*Contrary to what this image might imply, these horses are having a
friendly fight. The actions are considered friendly when
the horses' ears point forward.*

In Spain, there are two different styles of riding, both of which are widespread. Many of the purebred Spanish horses are trained in both styles. The Doma Vaquera style is used by Spanish cattle herders and bullfighters. In this style, riders rely on the transfer of body weight to maintain their balance. The reins are held in the left hand, leaving the right hand free to work with the cattle. However, the Andalusian is the true master of the Alta Escuela style. This is the classical Spanish Riding School method of movement for which these horses have a natural talent. The intelligence and capacity of the Andalusians to learn is apparent in the ease and quickness with which they master dressage figures such as *passage*, *piaffe*, and the "Spanish trot." They are also admired for their ability to perform complex movements on command without a rider.

*A stallion tosses his head and reveals the beauty of his eyes and thick mane.*

*A young Andalusian colt full of the joys of life.*

*This little chestnut foal observes its surrounding curiously but feels safest close to its mother's side. When it is a few weeks older, it will risk venturing a little farther from her.*

*Two Spanish-Anglo-Arabian mares graze with their foals.*

*A mare grazes in a meadow of flowers.  Her foal is only three hours old.*

*The young foal is already interested in its surroundings but remains calmly on its side until the time is right for further adventures.*

Andalusians are ideal riding horses. They are more suitable for people who want an intelligent horse for recreational riding or dressage than for competitive sporting activities, such as polo. As a result of a tough upbringing in their native country and their minimal food requirements, Andalusians are relatively easy and low-cost animals to keep.

*A gray stallion enjoys a meal of tender springtime flowers.*

*This stallion appreciates the fragrance of the fresh green grass and flowers, but his eyes and ears are always on alert to what is occurring in his surroundings.*

*Peaceful Andalusians are aware of their environment but are usually not disturbed by people who approach.*

*A coveted bay stallion makes the most of his freedom in sun-drenched meadows.*

*A closer portrait of this Andalusian's beauty as he stops for a rest.*

*Andalusians are admired throughout the world for their elegance and strength.*

# GLOSSARY

**bay** — reddish brown in color.

**breed** — (n) animals having specific traits; (v) to produce offspring.

**chestnut** — reddish brown in color.

**colt** — a male horse under the age of four years.

**crossbreed** — to mate a male of one breed with a female of another.

**dressage** — the art of training a horse to perform certain movements.

**foal** — a newborn male or female horse.

**gait** — a way of walking or running.

**gallop** — a fast way of running by an animal, such as a horse.

**graze** — to feed on grass or other plants.

**herd** — a number of animals of one kind that stay together and travel as a group.

**mane** — the long hair around the neck of a horse.

**mares** — female horses.

**reins** — long, narrow straps used by a rider or driver to control a horse or other animal.

**stallions** — mature male horses used for breeding.

**temperament** — the emotional make-up of a living thing; having certain traits, such as calmness or aggressiveness.

**thoroughbreds** — animals that are bred from the best blood through a long line.

# MORE BOOKS ABOUT HORSES

*All About Horses.* Marguerite Henry (Random)
*America's Horses and Ponies.* Irene Brady (Houghton Mifflin)
*Complete Book of Horses and Horsemanship.* C. W. Anderson (Macmillan)
*The Great Book of Horses.* Catherine Dell (R. Rourke)
*Guide to the Horses of the World.* Caroline Silver (Exeter)
*Horse Breeds and Breeding.* Jane Kidd (Crescent)
*The Horse and Pony Manual.* David Hunt (Chartwell)
*Horses and Riding.* George Henschel (Franklin Watts)
*The New Complete Book of the Horse.* Jane Holderness-Roddam (Smithmark)
*Wild and Wonderful Horses.* Cristopher Brown, ed. (Antioch)

# VIDEOS

*The Art of Riding Series.* (Visual Education Productions)
*For the Love of Animals: Horse Care and Ownership.* (GCG)
*Horses!* (Encyclopedia Britannica)
*The Mare and Foal.* (Discovery Trail)

# PLACES TO WRITE

Here are some places to write for more information about horses. When you write, include your name and address, and be specific about the information you would like to receive. Don't forget to enclose a stamped, self-addressed envelope for a reply.

National Association for Humane
    and Environmental Education
P.O. Box 362
East Haddam, CT  06423-0362

Horse Council of British Columbia
5746B 176A Street
Cloverdale, British Columbia
V3S 4C7

Pennsylvania Horsebreeder's
    Association
701 East Baltimore Pike, Suite C1
Kennett Square, PA  19348

# INDEX